CANCER SURVIVOR THROUGH FAITH

BASED ON A TRUE STORY!

SARAH ELISABETH ANDERSON

authorHOUSE®

AuthorHouse™
1663 Liberty Drive
Bloomington, IN 47403
www.authorhouse.com
Phone: 1 (800) 839-8640

Published by AuthorHouse 02/28/2019

ISBN: 978-1-5462-6636-5 (sc)
ISBN: 978-1-5462-6635-8 (e)

Print information available on the last page.

This book is printed on acid-free paper.

DEDICATION

I dedicate this book to my beautiful baby girl Navayah L'Faith Mayfield. If it wasn't for me being pregnant with you, I wouldn't have been here today. Thanks for saving my life! God knew exactly what he was doing when he allowed you to grow in my belly. Not only did I have to with stand "the test" you did too. Because we were both connected and God knew you before you were even born He knew that you would match my "BLESSED". Thanks for being strong while growing in my stomach! Even now as a young girl your brilliance continues to amaze me. I appreciate you for being the other end of my strength. When I wanted to give up I not only looked to God but he gave me you to look too, which reminded me every time that I needed to pass this test and show you the greatness of the Lord. Daughter, I love you and if I could give you anything in this world, it would be my FAITH in God. Whenever it seems that things are not going the way you think it should or could go remember to always "Faith your way through it."

CONTENTS

INTRODUCTION

As a little girl, I always dreamed of becoming a model, massage therapist, gospel singer, and be the best lovable person I could be. As I look back on my life, I can honestly say my mom made sure her children were safe and had everything we needed. Notice I am emphasizing *"needed"*. We were well fed, dressed, and attended church every Sunday. Growing up in St. Luke Church of God in Christ, in Moorhead, Mississippi, I sang in the children's choir where, Mother Lela Howard made me lead my very first song, *Thank You for Your Love* by the Mississippi Mass Choir. Although I felt nervous, it only assured me that I never wanted to sing in front of anyone any more. I was a very shy child, believe it or not. At the age of nine, my mom and I moved to Chicago so that my mom could fulfill the purpose God had for her life. I did not fully understand the role God played in the lives of His people until I became an adult and had to face my own trials and tribulations. My childhood and mid-teen years were great times. I knew I was loved. My life was great and filled with a promising future. I was blessed to get an all-expense paid trip to Ghana, West Africa because of my academic excellence at Marshall High School. I was often viewed as "the favorite" where ever I went, whether school, church, doctor's office, or just a gathering with friends. Despite all the good times, my personal tribulations and trials were about to take me into a new realm of experiences. This is where my faith story begins.

THE BEGINNING

When my parents named me Sarah Elisabeth, I never imagined that I would receive an assignment that would cause me to live out the calling of the meaning of my name. Sarah means princess in Hebrew and Elisabeth means *consecrated/devoted to God* in French, Greek, and American. It now makes sense to me why naming of children is so important. However, I don't believe my mom and dad, Carol and Leroy Anderson, even knew that we, as a family, would encounter the experience through which God was about to prove himself faithful. Nonetheless, this Princess Consecrated to God was being prepared to go through an unimaginable challenge. It was a life or death situation that could have turned out a whole lot differently than it did in the minds of many who may not understand the supernatural existence of Jehovah God. I advise every new parent to consider the meaning of their children's names because it points them in the ways of their destinies. Oftentimes we, children, will act like what we have been called. I know I tried my very best and was treated like who my name said I was, but that's another story for another book.

Ecclesiastes 12: 1 (KJV) admonishes us to *Remember now thy Creator in the days of thy youth, while the evil days come not, nor the years draw nigh, when thou shalt say, I have no pleasure in them;"*. As noted earlier, my mom had my brothers and me in

Church every Friday, Sunday, and Sunday night. I will always remember my days in Sunday School and Sunshine Band while at St. Luke Church. This is where the shaping of my faith in God began as a small child. I reflect on those humble beginnings and say, "WOW!" Everything that happened in my life was preparing me for what was about to come. Moving to Chicago with my mom and being introduced to a new church family – People's Church of the Harvest Church of God in Christ – would only serve as an opportunity to grow. Pastor Michael Eaddy, who is like a father to me, took me in immediately and began instilling his wisdom in me. As a young person, I began very early respecting the wisdom of the fathers and mothers who had the rule over my life, albeit, I disobeyed from time to time. You know how we young people do, don't you?

While attending school at Roswell B. Mason… I told you all I was "the favored" child in many of my circles… my former principal, Dr. V. H. Davis, and former assistant principal, the late Ms. Ruth B. Life, treated me like I was so very special. Whatever I needed for school, they would make sure I received it, whether they gave it to me directly or to my mom, who was teaching there at the time. I remember Dr. Davis giving my brother, LJ, and me presents every year for Christmas, although my brother was a *pistol* (smiling inside). I now realize that everyone whose life I entered was also meant to enter my life to help me live out the purpose I was destined to fulfill. God spoke in Jeremiah 1:5 - *"Before I formed you in the womb I knew you; Before you were born I sanctified you; I ordained you a prophet to the nations."* My journey did not truly begin until I understood this God-breathed statement about me. I hope each of us would realize just who we are and begin to walk the path of known destinies.

THE PAIN

Have you ever had a pain in your body that was so excruciating your body shivered to the point of no control? If you haven't, that's great news. If you have, then you will be able to relate to the pain I am about to describe. For two years, I can remember going back and forth to the dentist because I had such terrible, off-the-wall toothaches. For two years, my dentist kept telling me 1. You have an abscess on your gum and there's nothing I can do but prescribe you some antibiotics and pain medicine 2. You are so afraid that you make it impossible for me to do any work because you shake too bad 3. Come back in about two weeks after you have completed the prescription; hopefully, by that time, the infection will be gone. Can you imagine doing this for two years! Neither can I, but I did. As a child, you just do what your parents tell you and keep it moving. So, my mom was taking me back and forth to the dentist, still getting the same responses. I recall the last time she took me to see my "west side" dentist, I was shaking so bad, out of fear, I almost shook myself off the examining bed. This extremely abnormal shaking was used for my laughter later in the story. Never mind that, I needed answers to my dental pain and wasn't getting any at all. I kept saying to myself, "Who is this dentist that can never figure anything out?" From 2006 until 2008, I struggled with this pain. Let me clarify, the pain went from a level one to a level 10 and vice versa over those two years. You know how a toothache can do you. Some days the toothache felt unbearable and other days, after taking medication, you can kind of get along better and go about your days. Well, that's how it went over those two years. I continued going to school and doing the things most other teenage girls do – makeup, hair, dance squad, homework, tests, house chores, etc. It may have been my body was being protected by the pain pills. Who knows how I was able to go so long! I certainly don't know. Maybe it was an act of God. Whatever it was, the pain was intermittent, and I was able to live as normal as possible.

During this time (January 2008), my mom was transitioning our family out of the city of Chicago to south suburban Harvey. So, the excitement of moving out of an apartment into a house, took my mind off the pain! I was focused on helping my mom in our new beginning. After sharing a bedroom with my mom for the last seven years, I was finally able to have a room of my own again. Not only that, my brothers also had their own rooms. Alas! A four-bedroom house, out of the busy city streets of Chicago, was sure to take my mind off the pain for a while. Well, it did. I remember starting a new school – Thornton Township High School - at the beginning of second semester of the 2008-2009 academic school year. I met some amazing friends, teachers, and school staff. Some remain in my life to this day.

Well, it wasn't until June 2009, when I began experiencing even more weird and abnormal pain. This pain felt very different than the pain I had come to realize over the previous months. It felt more like someone trying to remove my teeth without providing me with any anesthesia and no pain medication. What a feeling! Although the pain was different, oddly enough, there were moments of relief where I could still manage without thinking this was life threatening. So, here I go again, moving on with life as normal as I could.

THE DOCTORS VISIT

As I stated earlier, I moved on with my life doing things that normal teenage girls do, right? I began feeling ill, abnormal illness – nauseous, loss of appetite, sick. My mom took me to see my primary care physician because she believed I was experiencing pregnancy symptoms. I recall walking in the bathroom to provide a urine sample and my mom asked if I had had my menses for the month. I told her that I had not. She stated, "I know something was out of order because the both us were pretty much following the same calendar." I took the sample back to the technician and my mom and I waited in the patient room for the results. The doctor came in and confirmed that I was expecting a child. At that time, I was at the end of my first trimester. Although it wasn't in my plan, I became pregnant during my senior year in high school. I won't call my daughter a mistake because I made the decision not to take the precaution to keep from getting pregnant. My actions were not foreign, and I knew exactly what I was doing. I didn't think about the fact I would or may become pregnant. Well, it happened. So, here I am, a senior in high school and with child. I came to the realization that I was pregnant; and abortion was not an option. I simply regrouped and began focusing on finishing up my high school education. I came to grips with the idea of how my life was about to change. I looked forward to meeting the challenges of motherhood head-on while preparing to graduate high school and go off to college. Well, those were *MY PLANS*. Jeremiah 29:11 –the Lord had plans for my life too. Those plans were to prosper me and not harm me and give me hope and a future. So, my plans became God's plan because I had to switch courses and get in HIS will. You will see that played out throughout the rest of this journey. Just because the clay deformed or became marred in the hands of the potter, it is no signal for the potter to throw it away. The potter simply makes it into something else just as beautiful. That's what God did and is doing with me. The journey isn't complete until destiny is reached. In October or November 2008, I began to have unbelievable toothaches AND headaches. The pain was so great, talking became difficult. In addition, I could not bear being in the room where there were lights on. The room had to be dark for me to be able to open my eyes and try to speak. My first reaction was that the aches were stemming from the pregnancy, so I called by obstetrician-gynecologist and scheduled an appointment to see her. I went to the appointment and had everything checked out only to be told there was nothing wrong and the baby was progressing very well. Even though she assured me there was nothing wrong with me relative to the pregnancy, I knew deep down within something was not right.

After returning home, I shared with my mom the symptoms and the pains I was experiencing. My mom recommended I go to see the dentist because my headaches may have been the result of my toothaches.

Here I am pregnant and in pain. I didn't have the foggiest idea what was going on, but I was not going to stop until somebody told me something. I am sure some of you can relate to what I am saying. So, here I go again. My mom scheduled me an appointment to see the dentist AGAIN! Tell me why this dentist tells me the

SAME THING AGAIN! He took x-rays of my teeth, told me I had an extremely bad tooth infection, gave me some antibiotics, and sent me home. He told me that the infection was the root cause of my pain. I went to the pharmacy and had the prescription filled. I made sure I didn't miss one single day taking my antibiotics like the doctor prescribed for the next seven days.

I will tell you this, I had the same results…

NOTHING happened.

The pain only got worse. It was then I urged my mom to find another dentist for a second opinion. I held on to the fact that there was something wrong. What did my mom do? She called 1-800-DENTIST.

Using this service, my mom was able to find another dentist with a reputable dentistry practice called Sonrisa in Chicago. Walking into Sonrisa, I felt very nervous but also felt relieved because I finally had that feeling that someone would be able to tell me what was wrong with me.

I knew I wasn't imagining this pain.

Was it psychological?

I didn't think so.

One thing I did believe was I am about to find out something. I had about a thirty-minute wait before the technician called me to the back to do an x-ray. After completing the x-ray scans on my teeth, I was told to go back up front to the waiting area until the dentist completed the review of my charts. Fifteen minutes later, the doctor called me back into the service area and shared with me the same thing my previous dentist had shared.

Well, go figure! He told me that he wanted me to take a different kind of antibiotic for the next five days. He wanted to ensure that the infection had cleared and scheduled me to come back to do another dental scan the following week.

I responded, "Yes, sir, I will see you next week."

I had a good feeling about coming to Sonrisa and seeing Dr. D. I wasn't sure what the results were going to be, but I knew they would be different than the rest of the results I had received so far.

I went home feeling better about my level of care that day. I began taking the antibiotics like the doctor ordered. I returned to see my dentist.

By now seven more days passed and I am about to get a follow-up examination of the teeth and determine the progression or regression of the infection. I signed in and waited patiently for the technician to call my name to be serviced for that day. After a short wait, I was called to the service area for a scan.

AGAIN, I was sent to the front office and asked to wait. This time it was about a forty-minute wait.

I began to get very impatient. I was thinking, "Why is it taking so long?"

Suddenly the dentist opened the door and asked for both my mom and me to come to the service area. His look was kind of puzzling because I didn't quite know what he was about to say. I can still see those x-rays he put up for my mom and me to see as he was talking. (I wished I had requested a copy of them for this book). He pointed out the x-ray from the previous visit and noted that there were still bone intact. However, he pointed at the x-ray from the current day's visit and all the bone was completed gone.

His words to us were, "I have never seen anything like this before."

He continued to say, "This is not something I can handle due to the nature of the progression of the bone dissipating."

He went on to explain that what he was looking at was beyond normal dentistry and a specialist was warranted.

Dr. D promised to do everything within his power to assist with scheduling the appointment. As we all know, it can take months to get in to see a specialist. My dentist was alarmed by what he saw that he went as far as making the phone call to the University of Illinois at Chicago College of Dentistry to speed up that process. He allowed us to fax the referral form to UIC as well using his leverage to reach out to speak with those in charge. Lo and behold, we were able to schedule an appointment for the following week to see a phenomenal specialist by the name of Dr. K., who now resides in New York.

Walking into the UIC College of Dentistry Maxillo-facial office, I was literally at peace. My experience at Sonrisa made the transition to the specialist easy and quite calming. Upon checking in with the front desk clerk, I proceeded to go and sit in the waiting area with my mom. By the way, if you haven't noticed, my mom has been with me all the way through the process. She didn't stop there, but you will see. Just keep reading.

Okay, let's go back to the doctor's visit.

After sitting there for a little while, my name was called to come to the back to one of the examining rooms. As I sat there, Dr. K and her team came into the room to look inside my mouth. She stated that a biopsy would have to be done to determine what the next level of care would be. Shortly, thereafter, Dr. K cut away a portion of the mass and told me that they would be running tests on it and would call me in about five days. She assured me the team would take the best care of me as they possibly could. She told me to just go back to school and resume my normal life and focus on having a healthy baby and graduating. That is exactly what I did. I returned to school as though I had not just had a biopsy done that left a hole in my gums to the point you could see the roots of my teeth. I tried to make normal appear as normal as I possibly could.

THE DIAGNOSIS

As I mentioned earlier, when I left seeing the specialist, I was instructed to go back to living my "normal" life. I told you I did everything in my power to do just that. Three or four days, post biopsy, I pretty much did the normal as much as I could. My mind was clear. I was back on track. So, here I am sitting in my finite math class trying to stay focused on finishing up the semester because graduation was becoming more of a reality. Right? Right. While sitting in my finite math class, suddenly my phone rings. Now, you know I am not supposed to be answering my cell phone in class. I jumped up and asked the teacher for permission to answer the call. He said, "Yes". I ran into the hallway and said, "Hello". The person identified herself as the nurse calling from the UIC College of Dentistry. She informed me that the results from my biopsy was back and it was important for me to come in to the office that day. I told the nurse I would call my mom and would be on my way after that because I had driven my mom's car to school that day. She said, "Ok, I will see you soon" and hangs up the phone. I immediately reached out to my mom to let her know what the nurse explained to me and that I needed to get to the doctor's office as soon as possible. My mom told me that it was okay for me to use the car to drive to Chicago. She told me I needed to go to the principal's office to inform the administrative team what was going on so that I could leave school. I went to the principal's office to get permission to leave school that day and commenced to go to see the specialist.

Leaving the school, I had no real concern about what may or may not happen to me at this point. I was happy and was going on about my day. I got into the car and drove down the expressway for about thirty minutes to my destination. I pulled into the parking garage, parked, got out and walked down the street to the building where the doctor's office was located. I knew where I was supposed to be, so I walked into the office, signed in, and waited to be called to the back to see the team. After a short while, someone came to the front and called my name. When Dr. K entered the room, she asked if I had come alone. I replied, "Yes, because my mom is at work." She stated that someone needed to be here with me during this time. Now, in my mind, things still weren't registering regarding what was about to happen. I was there with my mind wide opened to receive whatever news the team was getting ready to share. Dr. K directed me to call my mom and have her to come right away. She reiterated the fact that I did not need to be there alone, and it wouldn't be safe for me to leave the doctor's office alone. I did what she asked me to do, albeit unsuccessful. I called my mom several times, but she couldn't answer because she was lecturing at that time and was unaware of my phone calls. I let the team know that I was unable to reach my mom. So, someone from Dr. K's team ended up calling the college where my mom was teaching and asked to speak to her and that it was an emergency. The director of the education department went and got my mom to the phone at which point she was told to come to the doctor's office right away. The nurse from Dr. K's team informed my mom that Sarah did not need to be at the doctor's office by herself because the news was going to be devastating. My mom shared with me that she went back to the classroom where she was teaching so that she could alert the medical assisting department chair, Mrs. McClatchey. Since I had my mom's car, I didn't quite know how she was going to get to me. Regardless of the distance, some kind of way, my mom got to me so fast, it was unbelievable. I declare she got to me quick. She walked in the room with my God-sister, Felicia and Mrs. McClatchey, who also drove my mom to the doctor's office.

Now that my mom had finally made her arrival, it was time for the news. Dr. K took the two of us to a room, so she could share the news with us. I was extremely calm, still not understanding the graveness of the news that was about to delivered to my mom and me. I was cool, calm, and collected. Then, Dr. K, who was sitting facing her computer, opened her mouth and began to speak. She turned toward my mom and me and said, "Sarah, I am not going to sugar coat anything with you." "You have stage 4 head and neck cancer that is an invasive squamous cell carcinoma." "It is lodged in your right buccal cavity, your lower right jaw." She went on to say, "We are going to provide you the best care offered here at the University of Illinois Chicago.? My response was "Okay". I was simply clueless as to what all of that meant. I had never heard of stage 4 cancer. I did not even know, at that point, that this was a life or death situation for me. My mom broke out in tears and began cry because she had lost her father to head and neck cancer a few years earlier. Although I still didn't quite understand everything, I started to cry because my mom was overtaken with emotions. I could hear the enemy – the devil – speaking in my ear telling me I was going to die like my grandfather. He was telling me that it was my turn to die now.

Leaving the doctor's office that day, I still didn't understand what was going on. I had so many thoughts going through my head, so many emotions. The devil was beginning to put negative thoughts in my mind. I was simply muted the entire ride home. I was wondering what was going to happen to my baby. Let's not forget, I was about five months pregnant when all this news was shared with me. If I don't make it through this disease, who was going to take care of my child? What are the next steps after this diagnosis? So many questions going through my head, but not one time did I ask God, ***"why me"***. I remember thinking that I didn't want anybody to know about my diagnosis. I don't know if it was because I was afraid, ashamed, confused, or just didn't want anyone feeling sorry for me. I just wanted to get things rolling and get this over with.

The next day, which was a school day, I walked through the back doors by the lunchroom with a sad face. Every time someone would speak I would try to keep from crying because my diagnosis was on my mind heavily. I walked into the lunch room, which at the time was breakfast time, and there were my friends waiting for me. When we all see each other it was always hugs and kisses and talking girl talk. But not this day! Instantly they knew something was wrong with me. My friends asked all at once, "What's wrong?" And I replied, "Nothing. I'm okay". They knew I had lied because I was always happy and energized. They asked again, "What's wrong?" I then burst out in tears at the breakfast table saying that I was just diagnosed with cancer! Them not being able to understand what I was saying… they told me to slow down and breathe. I got myself together, wiped my face, and calmly said, "I was diagnosed with stage-four cancer." I can tell that each of one of my friends tried to remain strong for me, but we all sat the table crying and hugging one another as the bell rang for our first period class. This is a scene I will never forget. Here I am, at the age of 18, explaining to my high school friends about my cancer diagnosis. However, I assured them I would be fine and all I needed them to do was to pray for me.

Walking across the hall to my first period music class wiping the tears from my face, I knew that I still had a bright future ahead. With that in mind, I had to start thinking about lining up things for graduation. I had to update my graduation checklist. I had to prepare myself for the test God had set before me. I went to my teachers from my music, finite math, science, gym, English, and culinary arts classes to see what was needed for me to graduate in June 2010. Each of my teachers assured me I was passing their classes and offered to help me any way they could. They wanted me to focus on my health and my unborn child. My counselor at time pledged to do whatever she needed to do on her end that would result in my being a 2010 graduate. She reevaluated my transcript, updating it with the classes I had finished for that semester. Her response blew me out the water. She said, "Sarah, there is no need for you to even be here next semester any way." "You have more than enough credits and service learning hours to graduate." God already had things in order from school to the doctors to the care. It was all in HIS plan for my life All I could do was thank God and my counselor for enabling me to move forward without worrying about not being a high school graduate. After meeting with all my teachers and counselors, I said my good-byes to my friends and waited for my mom to pick me from school at the end of the day. Later that night I found myself sitting in my room praying and asking God, "What is it you want to do with me?" The Lord spoke to me and said, "I have to use you as an example for those who don't believe in my power." "You are the only one that can fulfill this test." I found comfort in what the Lord said because everything was in divine order. God assured me that he would never leave me nor forsake me. He was going to be with throughout the entire process. Nonetheless, I was yet wavering in my faith because this was a totally new experience. However, I accepted the challenge and the call. I had no further questions of God because it was then I began living my faith walk. All I could say was, "Lord, thank you for using me as an example. I am ready for the test". From that day forward, I walked with my head held high, a smile on my face, and boldly proclaimed my healing despite what was to come. For the rest of that night I slept like a baby.

Several days had gone by since I left school. I got a call from Dr. K stating that she wanted my mom and me to come into the office, so we can discuss the treatment plan that had been prepared for me. Getting to the doctor's office, my mom and I sat in the waiting area for about twenty minutes. We were then called into a conference room where we met with several doctors. This team of doctors included the oral surgeon, orthodontist, plastic surgeons, and oncologists. The team began to explain how the plan would be carried out. They discussed the best plan of care which entailed removing the cancer from my buccal cavity and everything that the cancer had deteriorated. The extensive surgery required was a total reconstruction of my jaw. This meant removing my leg bone (shaving the bone and shaping it like my jaw bone), skin, tissue, and veins, and the skin graft from my upper thigh would rebuild the floor of my mouth. My mom and I were shown a graphical prototype of the reconstructed jaw via the computer. The advancement of technology in medicine is absolutely appalling.

Dr. K and the team additionally explained that first things first. Let's not forget I was four months pregnant with my daughter. So, the focus initially was on my having a healthy baby. Once she was delivered, I would be able to spend only two weeks with her and the plan would be put into motion. At this point, I really didn't care about my life. I simply wanted to my baby to live. After the conference with the team, my mom and were sent home and attention was turned toward delivery of the baby.

THE DELIVERY

A month had passed since my last visit to the doctor's office to meet with the team of medical professionals. Around ten o'clock in the evening, I was awakened out of my sleep and heard the Lord saying to me, "Get up and put your baby's room together." At this point I was going on six months pregnant. So, I am talking to God like – "What do you mean get my baby's room together." "It's too early." I heard God say it again. "Get up and get your baby's room together." I was grateful for all the baby items that had been given to me at a surprise baby shower at my house. Out of nowhere I mustered up enough strength to get out of the bed and finish putting my baby's room together. I swept the floor, cleaned the walls, put the bassinet together, set up the changing station, put the baby clothes in the closet and dresser, stacked diapers and wipes against the wall by the changing station, and decorated the walls with Winnie the Pooh. By this time, I had worked up a sweat and became tired again. I had used all my energy obeying the voice of God, preparing my baby's room.

I knew I needed to take a bath after all of that moving around. So, I proceeded to go downstairs to run myself some bath water, take a bath, and try to get in the bed and get some rest. Because my mom's room was next to the bathroom, I went to close the door to her room so that the running water would not interrupt her sleeping. I got my wash cloth and dry-off towel and sat on the side of the tub until it was completely full. I took off my clothes, got in the tub and laid back so I could relax in the hot water filled with bubbles. I stayed in the tub approximately 30 minutes before I got out of the tub to dry myself off and head back upstairs for bed.

Wrapping my body in the towel, I opened the bathroom door and began to walk up the stairs. By the time I made it to the top of the stairs to the door of my baby's room, I felt some type of fluid running down my leg as if my water had broken.

I burst out with laughter because I just knew this was not real. My water broke...my water broke... oh my God!

With a smile on my face and without any pain, I ran downstairs to my mom, busted in her room saying that I believed my water had broken.

She woke up frantic asking me if I was sure.

I went into the bathroom, took a piece of tissue, and wiped myself so I could show my mom what was coming out of me. My mom confirmed that my water had definitely broken.

The hospital bags were already packed. My mom and I just had to rush and get dressed to get to the emergency room.

Let me remind you, I was going on six months pregnant.

Well, we got dressed and rushed into the car, and headed to the west side of Chicago to get to UIC Hospital. We went through the emergency room. Checking in, I informed the medical receptionist that my water had broken. She put me in the OBGYN room immediately so they could check to see if I had dilated as well as to determine what was going on. Being informed also of my new diagnosis of cancer and everything that was going on, the doctors, nurses, and other medical staff were completely puzzled as to why my water had broken. While they were being amazed, all I heard was God speaking to me saying, "Now is the time to get things started." I smiled and said, "Ok."

After being in the OBGYN room for nearly 30 minutes, a doctor finally came in to check to determine if I had begun to dilate.

Unfortunately, I had not.

This created even more confusion for the doctors because they couldn't understand why my water bag (amniotic sac) had broken.

After being made aware of my health situation, consulting with my oncologists, and running several tests, it was decided that I should be admitted into the hospital.

This was toward the end of January 2010.

The doctor informed me that the transport staff was on its way to take me to my room on the labor and delivery floor. My mom was walking beside the bed while I was being wheeled to my room.

When I got to the floor, I noticed how beautifully decorated the room was, bursting with bright colors.

The décor of the room got my attention immediately.

There was mini-baby lying on the bed, a flat screen television, nice sized bathroom, dining table and chairs, and a lazy boy chair.

The room brought forth so much comfort, but simultaneously, I knew that things were about to get very real for me.

As the transporter transferred me from the transport bed to the more comfortable bed in the room, she (the transporter) wished me luck and waved good bye. I will never forget her kindness to me in that short amount of time.

Well, I finally got settled into my room on the labor and delivery floor at University of Illinois Chicago Hospital. I slept very well that evening and peacefully, I might add.

You know how it goes. As a patient in the hospital, you don't get the opportunity to remain in a peaceful state. So, in comes the prodders and pokers (smiles).

Around 10 a.m. that morning I could hear one of the doctors discussing my big surgery that was scheduled for the month of February 2010.

The doctor continued to talk about inducing labor or having a C-section. On one hand the doctor felt my having induced labor and natural birth would be better because the healing process would not take as long. On the other hand, having the Caesarean would be a quicker process to remove the baby, but it would be a longer healing process.

I was lying there listening to the obstetrician-gynecologist and orthodontist debate about whether the process should include natural child birth or a C-section. However, understanding the extensive nature of my surgery, the doctors decided on the induced labor with natural child birth because this would make the process more bearable for me.

After deciding to move forward with inducing labor and giving birth naturally, the process to deliver began. Oh, medically induced labor started after my water broke, which is a natural form of labor inducing. This was something I had never experienced before, so I didn't quite know what to expect. Six hours after being induced, my labor nurse came to check in to determine if the medicine was working. At that point, I was not having any pain at all. She informed me that it would take about 24 hours for Pitocin to work.

You know what I did? I know you don't know, so let me share with you what happened. I went to sleep. When I woke up the next morning, I was "*starvin' like Marvin*" as the old saying goes. Well, to my disappointment, I was not able to get anything to eat. I could only crunch on ice chips. The nurse informed me that no eating was allowed during labor.

Wouldn't you know. The Pitocin did not work.

So, the doctor tried another medication to induce labor.

That one didn't work either.

So, now I have been induced using two different medicines while lying in the hospital bed for more than 3 days.

Finally, the foley Balloon catheter was inserted to help the cervix to mechanically open and then coupled with Pitocin.

Within four hours I began to feel contractions, but the pain was manageable.

The nurses and doctors were monitoring the contractions on the chart.

From what the doctors were explaining to me was that the chart was showing that I was having major contractions, but I was experiencing minor pain.

Those two events did not match.

Nonetheless, the two finally met up with each other and oh the pain!

The pain got so excruciating, I sat on the side of the bed shaking like a *leaf on a tree.*

I turned and looked at my mom as she was sitting on the recliner, voice trembling, and told her to please go and get the nurse.

I said, "I want an epidural because this is too much pain."

I continued to sit on the edge of the bed when my left the room.

I was praying that she would hurry up and bring someone back that could take this pain away.

Yes, the pain was just that bad!

My mom got the nurse right away. The nurse asked me to describe the level of my pain on a scale from 1-10. I immediately told her it was a 10 with no further information given. The nurse had me to lie on my back so that she could look at the monitor and to determine the length of my contractions.

Although it was only ten minutes, it seemed like an hour for the anesthesiologist and the nurse to come back.

The anesthesiologist had me to sit on the edge of the bed while he got the tools needed to place the needle in my back.

Sitting on the edge of the bed with my head down, shoulders relaxed, gown opened from the back, the anesthesiologist began to sterilize the area where the IV would be placed.

As I sat comfortably on the edge of the bed, I could feel the burst on my back which was the numbing medicine used to keep me from having to feel the pain of the needle.

The anesthesiologist warned me not to move while he was inserting the needle in my back. I was as still as a board of plywood.

After the needle was securely placed in my back, I laid back down and fell asleep for a few hours.

Awakened out of my sleep, I felt as if something was trying to come out, and oh boy was I right. I was alarmed! So I got on up and told my mom to look between my legs and see if she see the head coming out. With fear in her voice she said "girl no I'm going to go and get your nurse" I laughed out loud and said "ok" with excitement. As the doctors, nurses, and mid wife come running into the room, I was told to lift both legs so they could see in fact if I was really about to deliver.

I was fully dilated and ready to start pushing. The medical staff lifted me up and put one of those blue mats underneath me to ensure no afterbirth elements would get on to the sheets I was lying on. They begin to instruct and coach me through the process.

Remember, I received an epidural, therefore, I could not feel any of the contractions at that point.

I had to be told when to push based on the movement of the contractions chart.

Anyway, the nurse said, "Every time you feel a contraction (really didn't feel them, but the pressure), I need you to push and hold for ten seconds."

I replied, "Ok." First contraction, I pushed and held for ten seconds; second push the baby's head was at the opening of the birth canal (the vagina); third push, I delivered a 4lbs 14oz baby girl.

I was beyond excited to see such a bright, beautiful, healthy baby, my baby! She was premature by medical standards but was well on her way to being a large baby.

I recall the doctor holding her up and asking, "Are you all sure this child is only 32 weeks!" The medical team was awed by the presence of my big girl.

My daughter's name, Navayah, indicates a beautiful spirit. She had those beautiful brown eyes, thick, curly black hair, and round face, just adorable. She was my little princess. As gorgeous as she was, she came out with jaundice and had to have a bililight placed over her incubator to reduce the amount of bilirubin. This process would restore her color. She ended up staying in the hospital in the neonatal intensive care unit (NICU) for approximately two weeks.

Because I knew we would be soon separated, I visited her every day she was in the hospital. I breastfed her for the first two weeks of her life, which was very special to me. In addition, I recall one visit during which the unit sponsored a gathering of the mothers and fathers where we made artifacts that reminded us of our children who were yet in NICU. We did arts and craft, poster boards, and pictures that represented our love for our children. This was an amazing experience because we were able to take those artifacts home with us. I still have mine today.

On February 12, 2010, I received an exciting phone call from Navayah's nurse called to inform me that my daughter was well enough to come home. Mind you, Navayah was born at 32-33 weeks weighing 4lbs and 14oz. and the only problem she had was jaundice. She was coming home after being in the hospital for eleven days. I was so excited to receive such great news until I packed her diaper bag and caught the train from the south suburb to the west side of Chicago. I stayed until she was discharged later that evening.

Upon my daughter's discharge, UIC blessed me with several gifts for the baby such as breast pump to continue breast feeding, diapers, hand-crochet baby hats, baby bottles, blankets, and so many other gifts. I was ever so grateful for the gifts. The nurses took the time to show me how to nurse the baby and made sure all my questions were answered. As I signed the discharge papers, my mom called to let me know that she had set up the baby's car seat and was on her way up to assist me with getting everything to the car.

SURGERY TIME

It was so important for me to spend time with my daughter those last three days (February 12-15) because I knew I would be checking into the hospital on February 16, 2010. Those days leading up to my surgery preparation were critical to the mother-daughter bonding opportunity. I didn't know what to expect, but I knew my time was limited.

Despite the uncertainties, I was happy to know that my support system was intact and ready to pitch in to ease my mind. My mom, Carol, my dad, Leroy and two of his best friends from Mississippi, my aunt, Maderitrick and uncle Albert were all at the hospital with me prior to my going into surgery. It wasn't until then, while sitting in the hospital room, surrounded by my family, that things became all so real for me. However, I had no worries at all. I was simply ready to get things started so it could be finally over with. As my family left me at hospital, the room was suddenly quiet.

My mom drove everyone back home to ensure things were situated so she could get back to the hospital with me before my surgery.

The following day, February 17, 2010, the doctors woke me up around 5 a.m. and told me that it was time for me to get ready for surgery.

At that moment, I called my spiritual father, Pastor Michael Eaddy, so we could talk and pray before I went into the operating room. As Pastor Eaddy ended our prayer and before we said our good-byes or see you later, I told him thanks and ensured him I would see him on the other side. As we hung up the phone, the medical team came back into my room ready to wheel me into the OR.

Unlocking the latches on my bed, I was wheeled down the hallway with my mom walking alongside my bed. I smiled because I knew within myself I was ready for 'THE TEST'. As we get to the restricted double doors, which were for employees and patients only, I had to part ways with my mom. I handed her my eyeglasses, told her that I loved her and that I will see her after the surgery.

As the doors opened and we entered the waiting area before going into the OR, I could see my mom looking through the glass of the restricted area, ensuring I was okay. I looked back at her and threw her a kiss as she walked away.

As I awaited my time to go in to surgery, I was lying there in the bed in a holding area. A nurse soon entered and informed me that she was about to insert a type of medicine, they call "*a martini*", into my IV. She let me know that it was going to make me calm prior to my going into the OR. I replied with an okay. About five or ten minutes later I was told that the OR was prepped and ready for me.

As I was wheeled back into the operating room, I remember the nurse telling me to transfer from my bed to the operating table. I got onto the operating table and remember getting extremely cold. I was so cold I began to shiver. I was blanketed and made to feel comfortable as possible. The anesthesiologist came into the operating room, administered the dosage into my IV and within a matter of minutes it was LIGHTS OUT!

THE SURGERY (BEWARE GRAPHIC PHOTOS)

My doctors explained everything that had gone on throughout my surgery. I was out of it completely. The nature of the surgery was quite extensive.

The next few pages provides a glimpse into what I had to go through to remove the cancer from my mouth and begin the healing and restoration phases.

I cannot begin to share with you just how good God is and how His faithfulness to me increased my faith.

After enduring 23 ½ hours of surgeons removing the cancer, removing the bone from my leg to reconstruct my jaw, to sewing me back up to my waking up and living to tell about what was told happened to me, I can only tell you that I experienced a FAITH-BASED MIRACLE.

Each of the pictures in the graphical presentation provides some insight as to what the doctors did from a surgical perspective.

Image 1 is the neck dissection. This is an actual cutting open of my neck to remove the lymph nodes that were being tested to see if the cancer had begun to spread. After analyzing seven of the lymph nodes, cancer had spread to two of them, per my doctors.

As shown in Image 2, the cancer was removed along with my lower jaw, lower teeth, floor of my mouth, vein, pieces of my tongue, and lower gum.

After the removal of the cancer, my plastic surgeon, Dr. A, and her team began the reconstructive portion of my surgery.

Images 5 and 6 show how the team cut my leg open to remove the fibula.

They removed the bone.

They then shaved the bone to reconstruct my jawbone that was destroyed by the cancer.

Dr. A used the skin, muscle, and vein to replace what had been removed from my mouth.

It is a known fact that part of my leg is now located in my mouth.

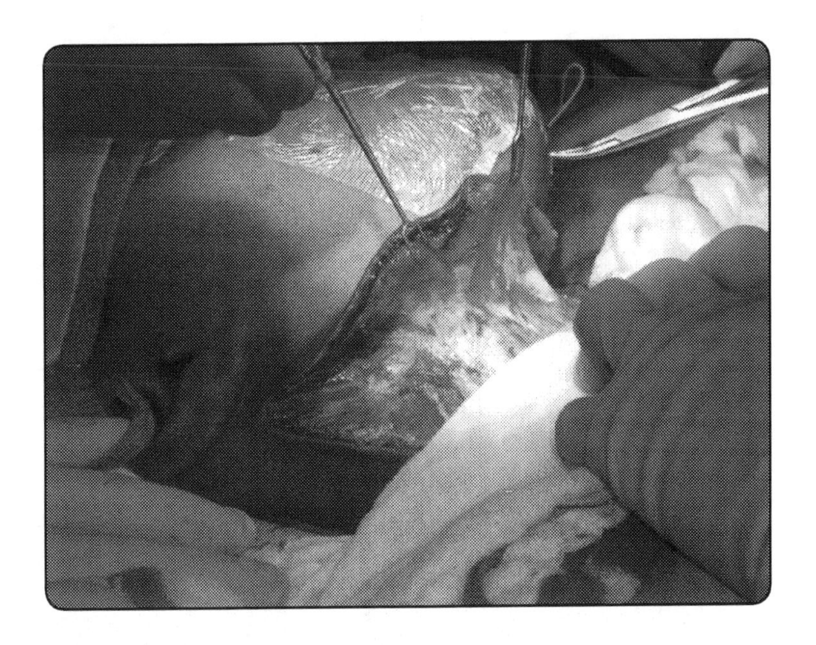

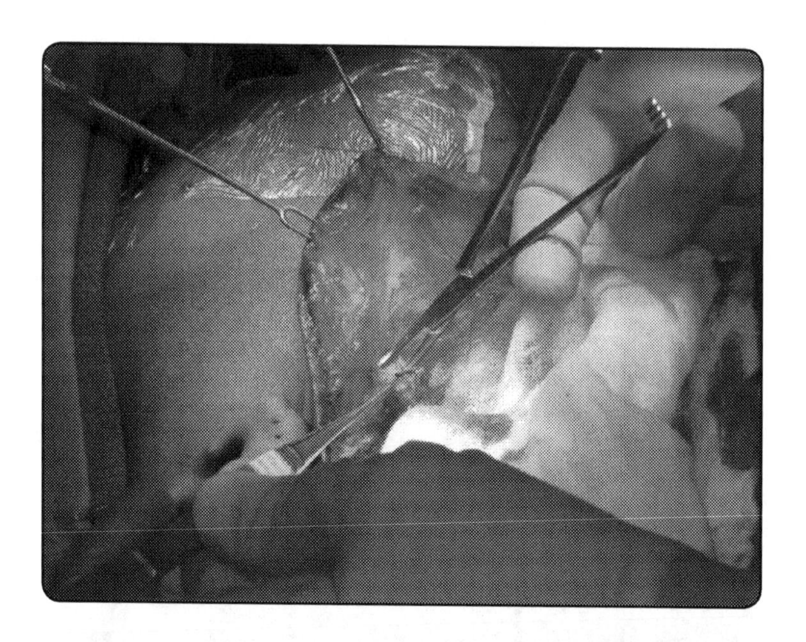

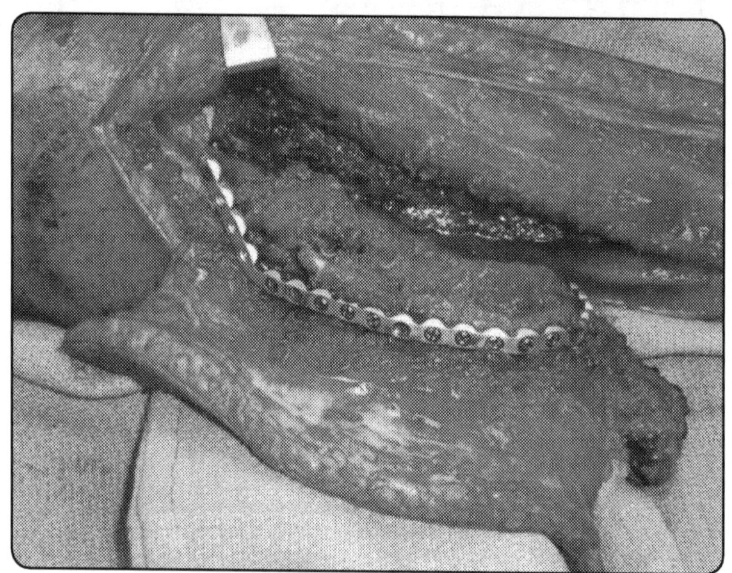

It is not just a figure of speech when I say that my leg is a part of my face.

When I say, "God is good", I really mean it.

It was nobody but God who could have allowed me to go through two major surgeries on the same day at the same time and come out alright.

After the surgeries were done the doctors then began to finalize everything by stitching me up, removing skin from my thigh to graft to my lower right leg. My leg was then wrapped and put in a cast so that it would properly heal.

I was kept sedated for almost 24 hours using Propofol Diprivan to keep me in and out of conscious.

I remember finally waking up in the intensive care unit (ICU) not knowing how I ended up there.

I was clueless as to what had happened and questioned why I was there.

I had what was called a "bear hugger" around my neck and chest, breathing tube in my nose, 3 intravenous needles in my arm, pressure cuffs on both legs, heart monitor on my chest, a monitor on my stomach, and an oxygen level and blood pressure monitor on my finger, and draining tubes in head to remove access fluids.

I felt as though I had been tangled up and shackled, but, I WAS ALIVE!

Amid my excitement and thankfulness, fear began to rush into my thoughts and in my mind. The fear of death became the ruling thought. I got to the point of not wanting to go to sleep.

I was simply afraid I would not wake up.

Because I had so many instruments hanging off me, swollen tongue hanging out of my mouth, couldn't see, I didn't have the ability to say what I wanted to so.

I literally had to write things down which wasn't always comfortable.

I started asking for my mom. I wanted to know if she was in the room somewhere.

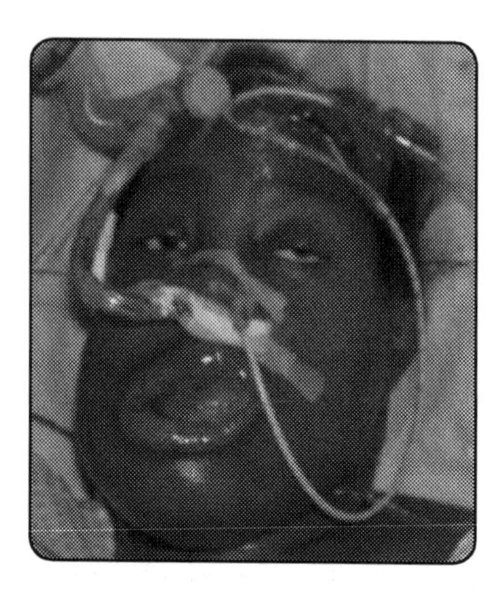

My nurse informed me that my mom was downstairs waiting to come up to see me. My fears seemed to have been getting the best of me at this point. My heart had begun to beat so fast I felt as though I was having a panic attack. My nurse assured me that everything was going to be just fine and explained the procedure I had just come through. She told me to calm down and that everything would be okay and helped me to understand what my next steps were going to entail.

I still wanted my mother, but no one was there to calm me down but my nurse, but that didn't take the place of my mother. I still wanted my mother. Are you getting the message? I still wanted my mother. I knew that whatever happened or would happen to me, my mom would be by my side.

Since I had begun to breathe on my own, the breathing tube was removed.

Finally, I was calm enough for the tube to be removed from my nose.

My nurse took the scissors, cut the stitches from my nose that were holding the breathing tube in place. She said, "On the count of three I need you to hold your breath as I pull the tube out."

She counted, "One, two, three."

I held my breath and the tube came out.

I coughed, gagged, and cried, and panicked because I had never felt anything like that ever in my young life.

I felt as though my life was being snatched away from me. Another nurse came in to assist the nurses who were already in the room to help calm me down. The only way for them to calm me down was to sedate me and that is exactly what they did. They gave me something to calm me down and eventually make me sleep.

There is nothing like the sound of your mama's voice during times of personal afflictions and crises.

I told you the nurses had to medically sedate me to calm me down.

I slept for a few hours.

After I woke up I could hear my mother's voice as she was talking with the nurse and getting updates on my surgery. I was not able to speak, but I was able to wave my hand back and forth to say hello to her. If you know my mama, you know she loves to talk and ask questions.

She asked me several questions.

I could only respond by writing things down.

I remember writing to instruct my mom to take pictures.

She asked me if I was sure that was what I wanted her to do. I replied, "Yes."

I knew pictures would play a major role in recalling what I had gone through.

So, my mom began capturing every moment of my process from that point forward.

When allowed to have visitors, different ones would come by to see me. I was still in the intensive care unit so there was a limited number of people that could come visit. I remember one day my God-father came by to spend some time with me. He put my hands on his head and asked me if I knew who he was. So that you will understand the significance of this touch, my entire head was still swollen from the surgery. I couldn't see anything or anybody, but I could hear. Anyway, after I touched his head and recognized who he was, he asked me to squeeze his hand for yes and lift one finger for no.

Will, my God-daddy, asked me if I was experiencing any pain. I lifted one finger indicating no. He asked if the doctors and staff were taking good care of me. I knew he would be highly upset and hurt somebody if they had not been taking care of me. I smirked while I was squeezing his hand letting him know that everybody was doing a phenomenal job in taking care of me. Lastly, he asked me if I wanted him to sing for me, and I squeezed his hand, to let him know I wanted him to sing to me. He began to sing *I Love You... I love you... I love you Lord today...* With his melodious singing, I ended up falling into a very peaceful sleep.

The next day, more of my People's Church of the Harvest Church of God in Christ family came by to see me. I remember Mother Whitfield, her daughter, Phaylor, my God-aunts, Shirley, Stephanie, and Marcie, and the Minister of Music, Sharon. By the way, did I tell you guys I was a singer? Well, I will tell you more about that later (laughing out loud).

But, I recall the minister of music came in. All I heard her say is, "I got the wrong room."

She literally thought I was somebody else. She was looking directly at ME thinking I was not who she had come to visit.

As she burst out in tears, I heard her say, "I can't do this." "Oh my God, I can't do this."

I kind of understood her emotions which did not really bother me, but I remember thinking, *everyone cannot handle me like this.*

I accepted that fact and came to grips with my new realities. I knew she loved me, but was unable to see me in the position I was in.

THE RECOVERY

After being in ICU for seven days, it was time for me to be transferred into, what was called, *the step-down unit.*

The breathing tubes were removed. I was breathing on my own.

I don't remember a whole lot that happened.

I was wheeled to step-down and placed in another room because my prognosis was better after surgery.

Spending minimal time in the step-down unit, the time came for me to now go home and begin the recovery process.

I was super excited about going home. My nurse came in with the discharge papers for me to sign, gave me the instructions on how to clean my wound, change the dressing, not brush my teeth, rinse with prescribed mouth was, and not to take a bath (only sit at the sink and wash up).

I was a bit distraught after the nurse told me I was not going to be able to get in the bath tub. I could only take a sink bath. Are you kidding me! I had been in the hospital for two weeks and not had a bath the entire time. I delivered a baby two weeks prior to my going in for surgery and was not able to take a bath then. I needed to take a BATH! So, I thought. The nurse repeated it again, "Sarah, go home, but do not get in the tub." I replied, "Ok."

Although I said, "Ok", I went home and did the total opposite.

I felt dirty and disgusting after not being able to be in the bath tub for over a month.

Yes, it was very nasty feeling. I was not accustomed to not bathing when I wanted to take a bath.

Anyway, what comes to mind is the old cliché that my grandparents used to say, *"A hard head makes a soft butt"*.

You know why? I will tell you that I did not follow the instructions given to me by the nurse.

MISTAKE, I must tell you.

I finally made it to the house, and you guessed it, I went straight for the bathtub. I turned on the shower and let the steamy, hot water run while I prepared to get in.

I know what the nurse said, but I felt horrible! I needed some hot water in my life (laughing about it now). It wasn't funny when I did it. I left the dressing around my leg where the bone was removed to reconstruct my jaw. I got into the shower and took me a shower. It felt oh so good!

Here's where the trouble starts. As I ended my wonderful shower, I bent over to turn off the water and began to feel light-headed. I finished turning off the water, stood up straight, and I immediately blanked out. I hit my head on the back of the tub. I had PASSED OUT! I was out for approximately two minutes.

Whenever you don't follow the prescription, generally things don't go as well as they could have gone.

There I was passed out in the bathtub with the door locked.

As I came to myself, I could hear someone knocking on the bathroom door as me if I was alright.

Although I heard someone, I could not respond!

I heard my mom asking my aunt if everything was okay, and my aunt said, "I don't know. She didn't respond."

That's when my yelled, "Open the door!" Of course, with the door locked, there was no getting in. My mom yelled again, "Kick the door open, unlock it or something, don't just stand there!"

My mom finally got the door opened and saw me lying in the tub semiconscious. As I said, I could hear everything that was going on, but I did not have the strength to speak. My mom picked my head up and cupped it in her arms trying to bring me back to.

She asked, "Sarah, are you okay?" I couldn't muster up enough strength to respond. She yelled, "Somebody call 911." Once I got enough strength, I told my mom I didn't want to go to the emergency room. She said, "Okay." She knew all along she was going to make me go to the hospital.

Shortly afterwards, the EMT came running into the bathroom to check my vital signs. My blood pressure had dropped tremendously low and, evidently, I was extremely dehydrated. As the EMT was doing their work up on me, my brother suddenly appeared out of nowhere to see what was going on. He knew I'd just gotten home from the hospital and wondered why the emergency services ambulance at our house was. By now everyone from the block was out on the street. While all the commotion was going on outside, I was still lying in the bathtub trying to convince my mom to not let the EMT take me to the hospital. I had just come home and did not want to go back to the hospital. She insisted on them taking me to hospital. That's exactly what happened.

Arriving in the ER, the medical staff at Ingalls Hospital took me straight to a room. A doctor came into the room asking question to get more history. She wanted to understand why my blood pressure was so low and why was my body so dehydrated. Even though I had been discharged from UIC hospital only a few hours with a stable prognosis, disobeying the instructions given to me by the nurse put on the road to a major setback. It may sound crazy, but I really enjoyed taking that shower. It landed me back in the hospital, but at least I was fresh. I felt that it was a shower worth taking. I know it's a little far-fetched, but I was feeling great! I got myself back on track and didn't take any more showers until the doctor cleared me to do so.

I stayed in the emergency for a few hours because the physician and team were working to bring my glucose and blood pressure levels up. I was unable to egest anything because of the swelling after surgery. The medical team had to come up with a way to break down the medicine so they could administer it through my feeding tube. Finally, something worked that would help me cope with the pain and bring my pressure and glucose levels back to normal. I will never forget the doctor who went and purchased a coca cola to pour down my feeding tube to regulate my glucose. Oh, how I wished I could have been able to taste that coke that day! All I did was burp loudly. Well, everything was back to a normal, coping state and I could now go back home and relax with my daughter for the rest of the night.

THE HELMET FITTING

I have been home approximately two weeks and now the time has come for the relaxation period to come to an end.

The check-ups, the fittings, the healing process is about to begin.

My first check-up after surgery ended with a great report and scheduled for the next phase – the plans for radiation and chemo therapies.

I went back to UIC about a week later to get my treatment plan. I was slated to receive three rounds of chemotherapy and 38 rounds of radiation therapy.

In addition to seeing the general oncologist, I met with the radiation oncologist and his team. I proceeded to the basement of the Oncology Center where I would be fitted for my radiation helmet. This helmet was worn each time I received my dosage of radiation.

I recall being summoned to the place where the fitting process would happen. My nurse asked me to get undressed, put on a gown, and walk to the first room on the left.

Walking into that room, I felt a cold temperature hit my face, and I became very, very cold.

It took about five minutes for someone to come into the room.

My nurse asked me to sit at the edge of the bed until she was done setting things up.

After about five minutes, she asked me to lay on my back. She used some type of laser tool to begin marking my chest with a marker, covering the markings with clear tape.

While completing the markings, my nurse told me to relax and asked me what type of music I liked to listen to. I responded, "I like gospel music." The nurse was a little shocked because very few of her patients ever asked her to play gospel music.

Most of her patients wanted to listen to jazz, R & B, or nothing at all. Because I wanted to hear gospel music, she got excited.

So, what did she do?

She pushed in the WOW Gospel CD!

It was after my nurse walked away to turn on the music I requested that I began to have a conversation with God.

THE TALK WITH GOD

This transformational experience was not an easy one for me in the beginning. However, it was not because I was not searching for answers. I wanted to know what the spiritual impact of this experience would be.

God, what are you wanting from me? Are you really here? I know you promised in your word that you would be with me always until the end of the world. But, God, how do I know you are here with me NOW? Is this your doing?

As the music continued to play in the background, I remember asking God, God, how do I know that you will be with me through this process. I prayed and I prayed and I prayed.

Before I ended my prayer, I asked God again, Lord, how do I know that you will be here with me in this process? Please send me a sign. I just need to know you hear me. By the time I finished asking the question, a song by Bishop Marvin Sapp came on in the background letting me know that MY MIRACLE was in MY FAITH. All I had to do was believe because my faith would move God to perform the miracle I needed for me. My FAITH was going to MOVE God to perform the miracle in my life.

The Lord explained to me in that moment that the only way I would make it through this test was to HAVE FAITH that HE would bring me through.

It was then that my question was answered and my faith was elevated. The Lord spoke to me through the words of this powerful song to help me focus on my faith and not my fear. Just like the woman with the issue of blood, all I needed to do was reach out and touch the hem of his garment IN FAITH and I, too, would be made whole.

My faith was no longer shaky. From that day until now, I learned and continue to trust God for everything. I had full confidence in the power of God and that He was here with me and would be with me throughout this entire experience.

I began to cry and went into full worship mode. I could not say anything but, "Thank You Lord" for affirming your word in my life. I was lying on the table being fitted for my helmet and found myself giving praise and worshiping God for who He was in my life.

During that two-hour period of the helmet fitting process, I cried, prayed, and worshiped God. It was on that table I made a real connection with God for the first time in my life. I felt like God had heard and answered my prayer.

Leaving the helmet fitting process, I was keenly aware that I had to walk through this journey my FAITH SHOES on while trusting God to walk with me and other times carry me.

I was excited to know that God had answered, but I was even more excited to know that my sickness was not going to end my life because God was to get the glory. As the New International Version stated it in John 11:4 - *When he heard this, Jesus said, "This sickness will not end in death. No, it is for God's glory so that God's Son may be glorified through it."*

I had to remember that this sickness was not going to take me out of the world because there was a greater purpose. I had to often remind myself that I am not alone because God was with me every step. No weapon that would come in to destroy would be successful. The Lord, my shepherd, promised to take care of me and not leave me defenseless.

The Lord assured me on that day that this was only the beginning of what was promised to be a journey of "watch God work". No matter how hard things may get, the Lord said, "Watch ME work." I cannot begin to tell you how the voice of God made a difference in this process.

I TRUSTED GOD and He, in turn, trusted me as HIS child with this sickness and this journey.

CHEMO & RADIATION THERAPIES

After the completion of the helmet, a few days had passed and was now time for me to have the port surgically inserted in my chest. This was the site of the chemotherapy treatment. It was amazing to watch the surgeon numb the location and make an incision in my chest to place the port-a-cath that would allow the chemicals to enter my body intravenously. He placed the port and then tested it to ensure blood was flowing through properly.

I was a novice at the phase of the process. I didn't quite know what to expect during this time.

After the port-a-cath was placed inside the upper left side of my chest, I was told it was going to take approximately two weeks for it to heal. Once the location healed, chemotherapy treatment would immediately begin.

I was scheduled to start chemo and radiation therapies about a month later. I was excited because the treatment phase was about to get underway. Why was I so excited? I thought to myself that the time had come to get this process started and get it quickly over with. Well, that was a huge mental error I made because there was nothing quick about this process at all. I mean NOTHING at all!

I tried to rush the prognosis! That was a mistake I would ask you to never make.

Anyway, during my first visit for my chemotherapy, I was called to a small room to right side of the corridor where my blood was drawn to check my white blood cell count, potassium, calcium levels, etc. I was then sent back to the front to the waiting area.

While waiting my mom decided to go to the lunch room at the hospital to get some food. I waited about 20 more minutes before the staff finally called me to the back. They began to check my vitals and prepped me for my first chemotherapy session.

The nurse walked me down the short corridor where she put in the key code to open the door. Just inside the door, she told me to step on the scale so she could record my weight and height, blood pressure, and temperature. Once all vital signs were checked and given a "clear", I was taken to the room to start treatment.

Walking into this private small room, I remember this light blue "lazy boy" chair, a monitor to which the medicine would be hooked to, a single chair for a guest, a chart on the wall, and a television. The treatment room was comfy and cozy.

It mattered not how comfortable and cozy the room looked, I needed to get plenty of blankets because I was always cold (lol). It didn't matter it was summer time. I was freezing!

As I made myself comfortable on the light chair, my nurse gave me two gowns to put on so that the port could be easily accessed.

At this point my mom had not yet come back from eating lunch and I asked if I could wait until my mom returned before I began treatment. The nurse confirmed that it would be okay to delay starting treatment until my mom came back.

I called my mom and informed her that I was in the back preparing for treatment but wasn't going to start until she walked back to the Oncology Center. That's when my informed me that she was getting off the elevator heading toward me. My nurse went to the front and escorted my mom to the treatment room where I was located.

My nurse and my mom came into the treatment room laughing at who knows what. I smiled and nodded at the two of them. My nurse then asks, "Are you ready for your first treatment?" I replied, "Yes, I am."

The nurse told me to lower my gown so she could access the port. She rolled in the preparation table that had sterilized gloves, port packets, gauze, saline, alcohol wipes, tape, and clear tape to cover the entire area after everything was cleaned and placed for treatment. She told me to lie back as she put on the gloves. She ripped open the alcohol pads and began to clean the port area.

My nurse informed me that "this may hurt a bit, but not for long". I braced myself for what may hurt. She pulled out this long needle and squeezed the two butterfly wings on the needle and stuck it into the port-a-cath.

Just as she said, IT HURT!

The sting lasted only for a few minutes, though. She then connected a tube of saline to make sure the port was working properly and that the flow was uninhibited.

Now that the port was working find and the flow was great it was time to stabilize the area, close everything up and connect the chemo treatment. Connecting the chemo treatment to my port, the nurse told me that most people either go to sleep, read, watch television, etc. to by-pass the time. It took about three-four hours for the first chemo treatment to be completed. That was a long time. The nurse cleaned up her area and brought me apple juice and gram crackers while I waited. After I finished my snacks, I went to sleep for the remainder of the treatment.

Waking up after my three hour treatment I felt no effects from the chemo. I was excited because the treatment wasn't as bad as everyone said, at least for that moment. Checking out of oncology and heading down stairs for radiation treatment, that's when reality hit me. I checked in sat for a while and waited for my name to be called to go to the back of the room and start radiation treatment. As my name was called and I was told to go in the dressing room and remove all my cloths and place a gown on and then after someone will be in to get me shortly. My mom stayed out in the waiting area as I started my treatment.

Knock knock Knock...There's a knock at the dressing room door. I answered "come in!" The nurse said that everything was ready for me to come back and start treatment. As I gathered my things, the nurse and I walked down the hall way into the radiology room I was instructed to lay flat on the table with my hand to my side while the nurse placed three heavy, comfortable warm blankets on me. I felt great! As I lay back comfortable on a pillow and tucked in very well, my nurse tells me not to move. yet he insisted that I should take a nap and by the time I wake up I'll be done. I was told that during this procedure I wouldn't feel not a thing but there will be side effects from this treatment. I replied with an "ok" as he stood to my right checking to see if my IV fluids were in fact moving at the correct speed for treatment. Maybe about forty mins had passed and Its time for my first radiation session to be over and again I felt very well, just hungry, which for me wasn't a surprise. My nurse came in a woke me up saying that treatment was over and to get ready and head to the dressing room and get dressed. While still laying flat my nurse begin to remove the IV from my arm so that I can get up and get going. As we said our see you later I walked out of the room and walked down the hallway to the dressing room so that I can return the next day.

Radiation treatment went on for another thirty-seven days. Although there were breaks in between treatments due to the side effects from chemo and radiation I had some really tough days. I was admitted into the hospital for having little to no fluids in my system, and even had to get three blood transfusion. Things where getting hard! Now that I was a little better it was time for my second round of chemo. This is when my side effects from chemo tore my body down. I began to lose my hair, my sense of smell was gone due to radiation therapy, I dropped down to 79lbs, and really began to go into a deep depression. Now that everything seems to be going from good to bad, I was in a place where I didn't want to be seen heard or even bothered. I wanted to get my treatment and head home. Yes, I know that things could have been worse, but for me this was the worse. Reason being is because now I can't eat, I'm losing weight, and things seems not to be working in my favor.

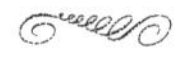

THE DEPRESSION

I told you that I made a huge mental error rushing my prognosis. It had become even more evident of just how naïve I was to this process and what I would have to endure.

Depression set in.

My world was getting dark and lonely.

As things appeared to go from bad to worse, I began shutting people out. I no longer wanted to go to church.

I didn't want to spend time with my family.

To make matters worse, my *friends* were already out of sight. That really hurt me! You know? After going through such traumatic experiences, you would think your friends would be there. That would not be the case. They were invisible. I realized, however, some people are in our lives for seasons and others for reasons. When their times are up, you must let them go. That was extremely hard for me to digest at the time, but I learned quickly.

Why did I become so depressed? Where was God in all of this?

Depression set in the moment I began focusing on MY SICKNESS and took my eyes of MY SAVIOR.

I did like Peter in Matthew 14 – as long as Peter focused on Jesus he walked with ease on a body of water. As soon as he stopped focusing on the Savior, Peter began to sink.

So, my sinking (MY DEPRESSION) happened when I switched my focus from FAITH to FEAR. I chose to resort to pushing God away instead of drawing nearer to Him during my hardest periods.

I stopped praying.

I stopped praising.

What I soon realized was DEPRESSION WAS NECESSARY! In my depression, I reached out and touched GOD who was ALWAYS there. He was my first love. In my alone time, I rekindled my relationship with God. He taught me some very valuable lessons.

How did I rise from this depressed state? It was the still small voice of God speaking to me during my solitary confinement. He assured me He was there with me. He told me He loved me. He told me, "Daughter, I need you to trust me, not people."

Because I was looking for people to do a God-job, depression overtook me for a little while. But, I am so glad God never left. He wanted me to look to Him. Tough love is the best love. Love's application may not always be comforting and soothing, but it will never leave you wounded.

My depression experience taught me that I had to learn to love the RECONSTRUCTED SARAH because this is the Sarah that will love God with all her heart, her might, and her soul. This is the Sarah that rely solely on God to take care all her needs. I learned to tell God about my problems and waited for Him to solve those problems.

My depression was necessary because it showed me I was simply talking ABOUT faith but wasn't living faith. God reminded me of His word in Hebrews 11:1 where the Bible states, NOW FAITH is the substance of things hoped for and the evidence of things not seen. In order to realize my healing, I was going to have to see it before the healing took place.

Depression helped my FAITH COME ALIVE!

My relationship to God, through my depression, helped me to reignite my faith. I began walking (living) by faith and not relying on what I could see through my natural eyes. Although I had experienced a bump in the road, it was only a distraction. God saw the best in me when everything around me was looking hopeless, dark, and dead. My lowest point elevated me to my highest point in God.

I gained supernatural faith abilities after going through my depression. It could have taken me out of here. I could have given up. I could have stopped believing God. BUT GOD!

LAST DAYS OF TREATMENT

Here we are at the last day of treatment and its time to say our good byes. One of the nurses had something very special she wanted to do for us right before Christmas time. One of the nurses asked me to write down at least five things I wanted for Christmas that year and she will see that I get it. On that list I wrote that I wanted a Wii, watch, and a purse. Just something small because at that point I really didn't know what I wanted for Christmas. In my house we didn't really celebrate Christmas as in getting gifts. So, I was sent on my way and didn't have to return to the doctor until another two weeks.

Two weeks had passed and its time for my regular check up to see how my tumor area is progressing. I went to the back and meet with Dr. Howard who is the radiologist and we did several tests and all results came back normal. Thank God for Jesus! I went back to the front after the doctors visit to tell my mom the good news and from there we went home joyous. Leaving the doctors office, we went home and ended the day.

Here we are at Christmas time at the holiday party for the radiology center, I meet so many new people and had a great time showing off my beautiful daughter which I had given birth to right before my surgery and treatment. I was excited and had a great time. We danced, we sang, we ate, talked and laughed. Getting towards the end of the party it was now time to open our gifts. I was handed three big boxes. And guess what it was? EVERYTHING I had ask for. I was in such amazed because all I could think of is “how can someone do so much for me”. I realized then that I had a team surrounding me that care. My entire team of doctor believe in God and walked by the same faith that I had. That’s what I love about God, when things are done in His time, all things will work out in our favor. We must be willing to go through the test when its time.

THE "HEALED" CALL

As my healing process was getting better, I was required to go to visit my doctors less. Instead of having to visit the doctors every week, I started seeing them once a month or every other month.

My diagnosis of stage 4 head and neck cancer was on its way to a better prognosis. At least, that was my hope and prayer.

It was October 2010. I remember receiving a phone call. My phone rang and rang and rang. I finally answered the call.

The person on the other end said, "Hello, this is Dr. H. from UIC radiology department." "May I speak with Sarah."

I replied, "This is she."

He said, "Great, because I am calling you to let you know I have some good news." "I wanted to be the one to call you myself."

I said, "Good news?!" "Okay!"

He said, "Yes." "I want to let you know that from all of the tests, blood work, etc., all of the cancer is gone and there is NO sign of your cancer EVER returning."

I screamed with tears rolling down my face and said, "Thank you Jesus!"

I could hear his grin over the phone when he said, "Yes, thank you Jesus."

We hung up the phone and all I could do was cry and thank God for keeping his promise that He gave me BEFORE the test.

From that day forth, I walked in victory with my head held high on my way to COMPLETE recovery.

RESTORATION PLAN

A few months had passed and now I have to go to UIC College of dentistry where I meet with a team of oral surgeons and a plastic surgeon so that they can come up with a restoration plan. In the beginning the plan was to restore the teeth that I had and place dental implants in the area where the teeth had to be removed. We began by filling all cavities which was on every tooth I had and restore the teeth. But, every visit I had the follow week the cavity was back in the are where it was just restored along with infections.

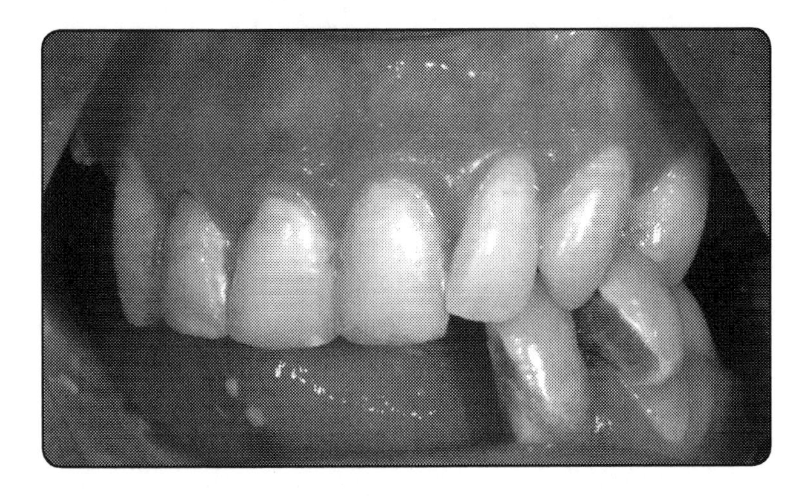

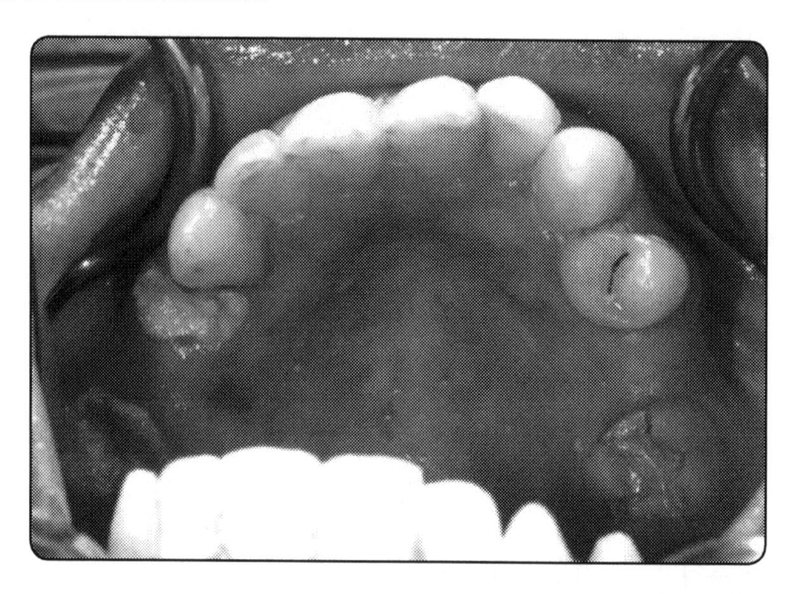

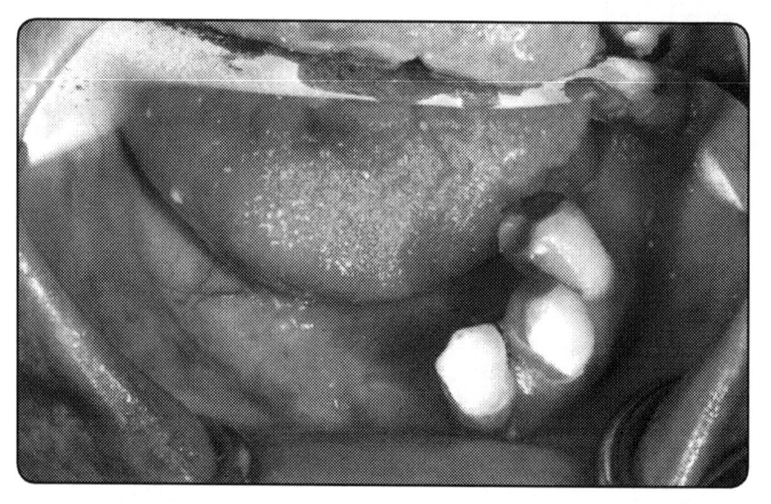

That gave the dentist a head ache. Nothing was working due to me having severe dry mouth from radiation treatment. Severe dry mouth causes bad breath, tooth decay, and infection, and at the time I had all of the above. Therefore, we had to come up with another plan. At this point I was passed of to the students of the college of dentistry to see what type of treatment plan they would come up with for a person such as myself and this type of case.

This is where I meet with Dr. P. Dr. P was very cool. I feel in love with her spirit right away. She was loving, patient, and real and most of all she wanted the best treatment for me! Going to a few doctor's appointments with Dr. P we tried so many different things to keep my cavities and infections under control. Until one day she came to me, and I can tell that she was very nervous asking me this question but she asked me, "do you mind if we remove all of your teeth and put all dental implants" I said "YES, oh my God this is what I have been praying for the past month because I couldn't take no more of my mouth being tortured by having needles and drills in my mouth all most every day. It was getting to be a bit too much. With relief she said "really? Are you sure?" I said "YES PLEASE!" With excitement she went to her boss and told him my respond and we then came up with a plan to have surgery, remove the rest of the teeth I had and place implants. This planning took about two weeks.

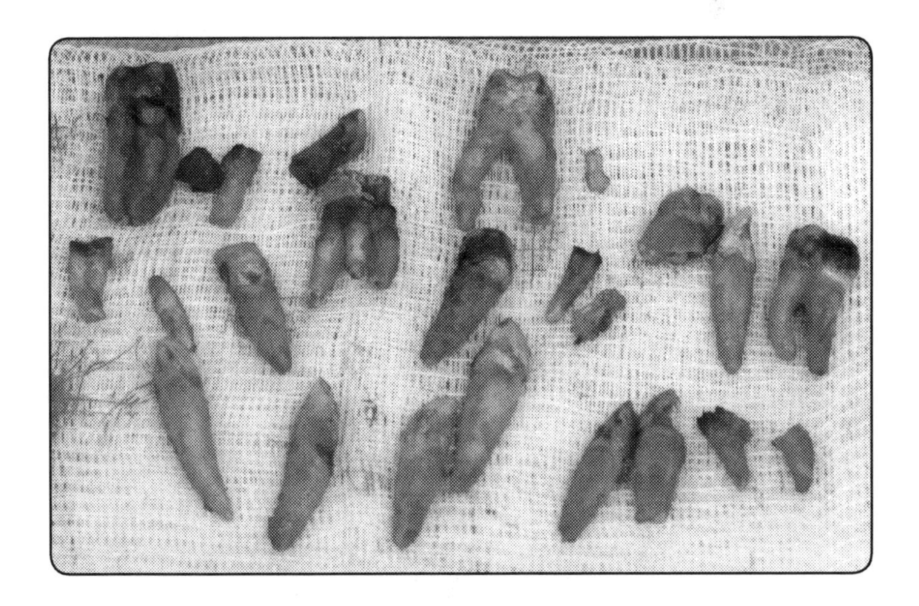

Two weeks had passed and now the treatment plan is in place. The plan was to remove teeth, place 8 dental implants, and create a cast for my upper teeth so that dentures could be made while I was in surgery. The dentures where going to be placed because they knew I was young and wouldn't want to walk around bald mouth. In fact, I would need something to cover up my upper mouth until my implants heal, which took about 6 months. Heading into surgery the treatment plan takes place and about two hours later I woke up in the recovery room with my mom by my side.

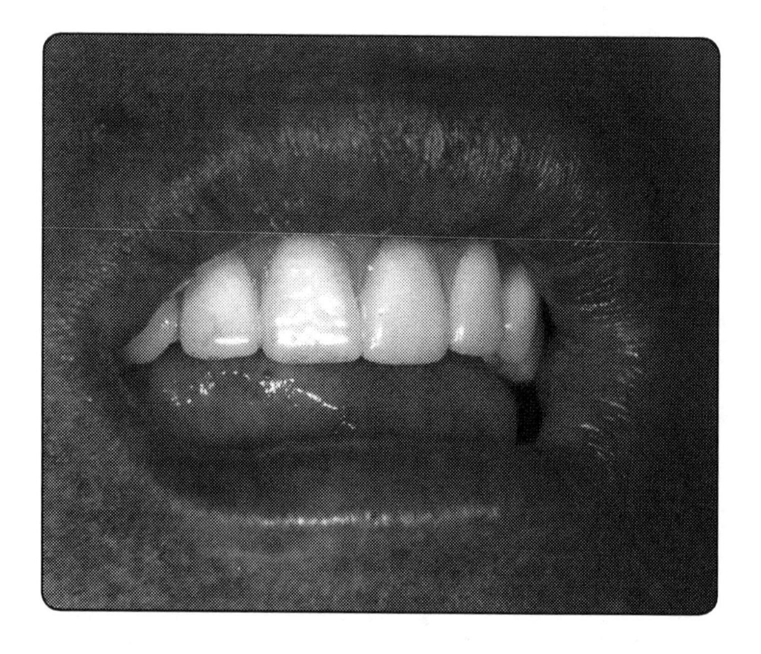

Up and ready to go home I left with a swollen smile on my face. Excited about what's about to get ready to happen. I knew that in six months to a year I will be back smiling and eating what I want.

About three months had passed and now it was time for me to go in and get and x-ray to see if the implants had gelled to my jaw bone correctly. By the doctor's surprise not only did the implants gel but the then found out my regular jaw bone on the left side had infused to my leg bone that was replaced to make the left jaw bone. That left the doctors in AMAZE! That day I had double good news.

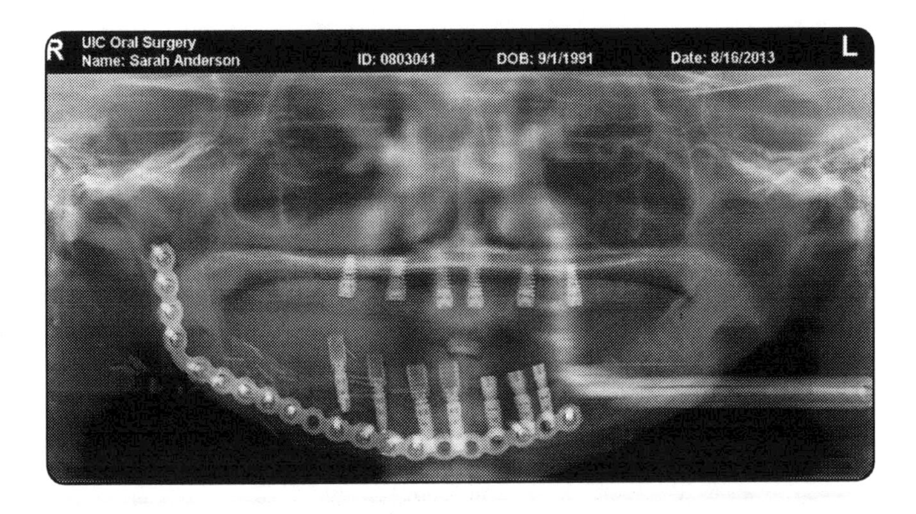

Now that the six-month healing period is up it is now time to go into surgery and do the uncover of my upper implants. During this surgery my gums where reopen to reveal the implants that was underneath, but because it was so much bone and gum loss I had to use donor skin to replace it. After surgery I had to wait another two to three weeks for my mouth to heal and for the stiches to be removed.

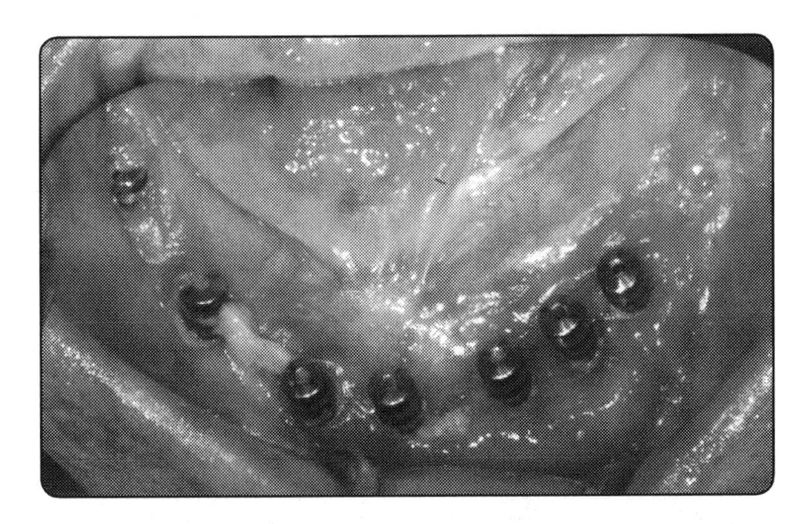

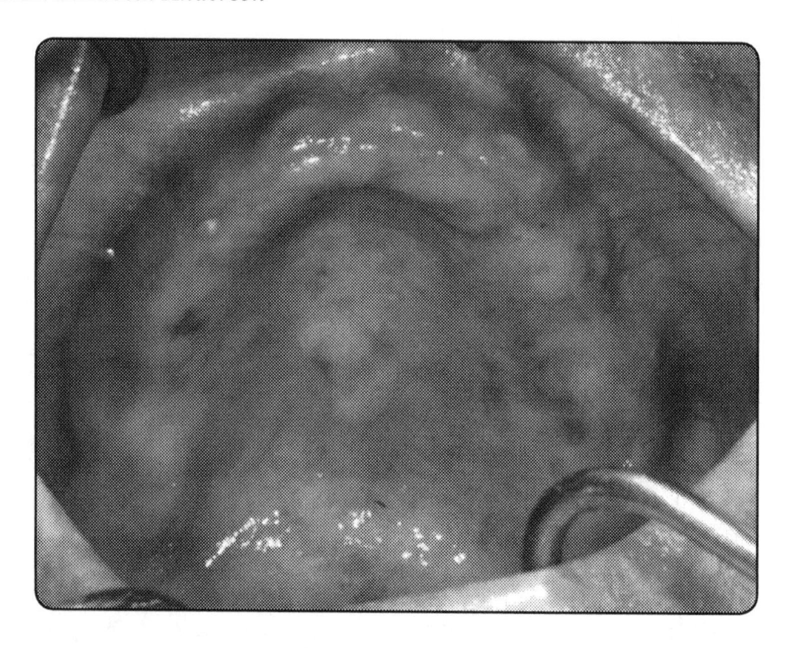

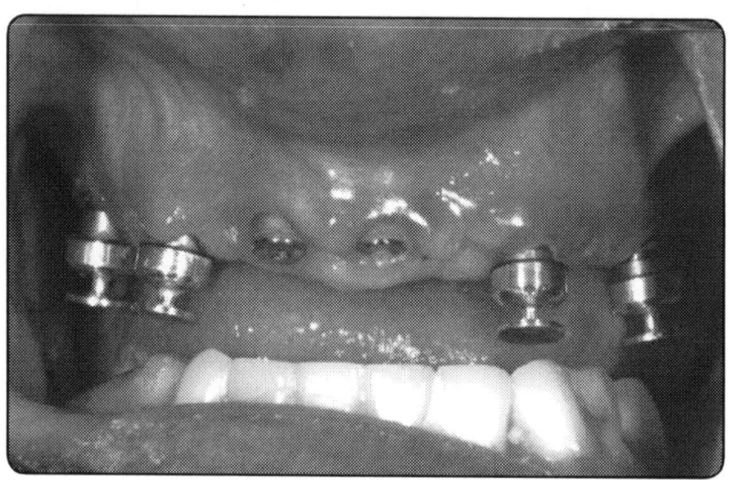

Now that my mouth has healed it is now time to do some impressions of my mouth so that my teeth could be created to be placed on my implants. This was the worst. I hated getting impression done but I knew it had to be done if I wanted my teeth before Christmas. While getting the impressions done and having the guard placed in my mouth for the fitting all I can feel is the thick blue and sometimes purple glue going down my throat making me gag and feel sick to my stomach, but no one said this process would be easy. I was so glad when it was over. Now that the impressions are done it was time to take them to the lab for the creation of my permanent teeth. Yes, the teeth I would have to wear for the rest of my life! Oh, the excitement I felt! All I want my doctor to do was to take a precious time and bring me back some perfect pearly whites.

I would go home and look in the mirror and just imagine how I would look with them. I would practice certain things I would say and just begin smiling at things that wasn't even funny. I just know that my teeth were being made and I didn't have much time to practice. But I made sure that everyday I woke up and cleaned my mouth for the day I would smile and practice certain things and though about the first foods I would try eating as soon as I got them.

Weeks and weeks had passed and I get a call from my doctor saying that it was time for me to come in to try on my first set of teeth. I jumped up with excitement because I new that I would have a new smile for Christmas. My appointment was scheduled for the next morning. The next morning, I checked into UIC College of dentistry and all I know is that I was very nervous and excited all at the same time. Sitting down wait for Dr. P to come out and get me I said a quick prayer and prayed that everything will work out in my favor. Here comes Dr. P walking around the corner to get me. She asked me how I was feeling and asked about my baby girl which she did all the time. Small talk! We walked to the back and sat at our work station and got ready to work. I removed my dentures and placed them on the table to be cleaned as she walked out to get the supplies she need to get this process started. I laid back in the dental chair ready to start everything because I knew this would be a long process.

Dr. P finally comes back with the supplies and my new teeth in a sealed bag. She asked me if I was ready to see if things worked out, I said yes with my gums showing as I smiled. Doctor P directed me to lye back while she pressed the automatic foot pedal and leaned me back to get things started. I was asked to open my mouth as Dr. P shined the ever so bright dental chair light into my mouth and began to work. First we had to make sure that my mouth was cleaned and ready t work. All thirteen of my implants were removed, cleaned and some was replace due to being loose, but it was n major problem. As I rinse my mouth out with mouth wash and water through the water pik it was time for the try on.

As I open wide, here comes the lower denture being placed in the floor of my mouth trying to correctly place them on the lower implants. Screwing in the abutments and getting out the upper denture and placing the abutments in its time to see if it's a match. We went through the fitiing and measuring process for at least an hour. I ten felt like something was wrong! Dr. P stated that something isn't adding up right with the measurement. She left the upper and lower dentures on and took a picture.

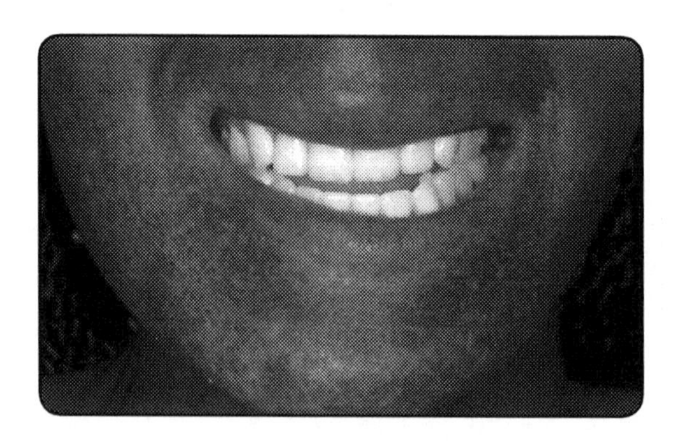

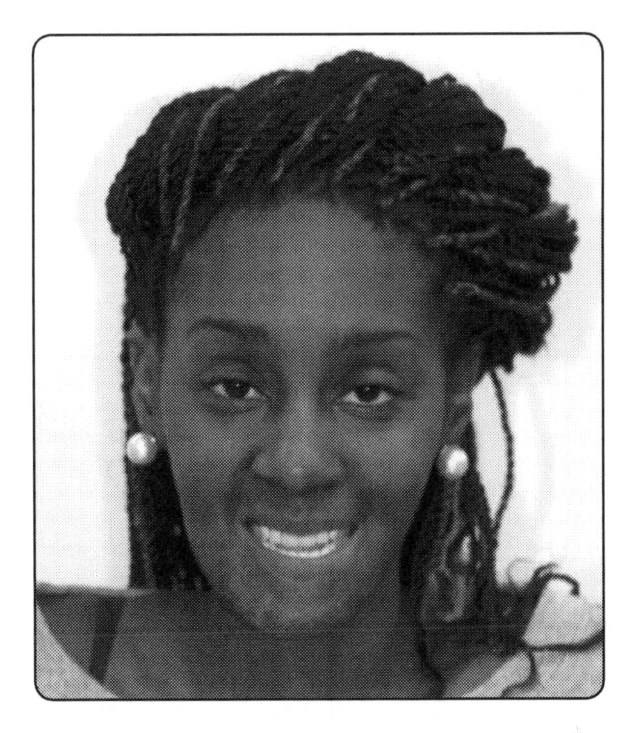

Looks like I wouldn't have my new teeth for Christmas this time. Leaving with a sad face and really hurt I felt like going into depression again. Lol but very serious. But there is a God who never seems to fail me. I get a call a few days before Christmas from Dr. P saying that she thinks she got the measurements right. So, I rushed in the next day a repeated the steps from a few days ago, and I finally had my permanent teeth! I was in love with my smile all over again and was ready to bite into my first pickle and my first cheese burger.

ROAD TO CONFIDENCE

What started as a toothache and ended up being stage four head and neck cancer (invasive squamous cell carcinoma of the lower right buccal cavity) helped me to grow and develop as a person, a friend, a daughter, a child of God. This sickness delivered a heavy dose of transformational and reconstructive remedies that would set me on a course unimaginable. The story is yet to be written and told.

A young girl who was timid and shy has gone through one of the most devastating experiences a teenager could fathom.

From 110 pounds to 79 pounds

From a head of long, beautiful, brown hear to a completely shaven bald head

From a mouth filled with teeth to a mouth with dentures and implants

It was a long road to recovery and many challenges on the way. However, in 2014, I finally began to accept who I was, what I looked like, and the example I was to set for others to follow. I accepted my calling, and God had prepared me for the journey.

I recalled being awakened out of my sleep one night. I heard the voice of God say to me, "Get up and put a video together highlighting my current prognosis. I didn't quite understand what He was trying to get me to do. I asked God, "God, what is it you want me to convey through this video?" "What do you want me to say"?

God gave me step by step instructions as to what to do put the project together. He reminded me, "This sickness was not unto to death, but it would be to bring glory to him." I downloaded a popular app called Flipogram. The Lord instructed me to pull certain pictures that had been taken to show the things I had gone through. He had me to place the pictures in a certain order.

He instructed me to upload my favorite song, at that time was I Don't Look Like What I've Been Through by Deon Kipping. I pressed play. It appears that the song and pictures were in sync. Yes, God is just that strategic!

I ran downstairs and let my mom watch the video to see how she would respond.

She was in tears.

I told her that God had instructed me to compose the video and upload it to Facebook.

Around 2a.m. that morning, I uploaded the video to Facebook and went to bed.

When I woke up around 9a.m. that morning, the video had reached almost 2 million views and 100,000 shares.

I was amazed at how following God's direction to do something like this would do for millions of people around the world. There were and still are people who NEEDED to see that video.

It is just as amazing to find out about the millions of believers who are wavering in the relationship with God because they lack faith.

I have learned that there are lost souls out there waiting on us to share the good news of Jesus Christ. God certainly got the glory because many testified about how this video encouraged them to rededicate their lives back to God.

Revelation 12:11 (KJV) noted that they overcame him by the blood of the Lamb and by the word of their testimony. I am grateful that my testimony helped me to overcome the enemy of fear, depression, low self-esteem, and self-pity.

I believe, just as God gave me that video to share with the people, that people are looking for ***authentic testimonies*** to which they can relate so they can be overcomers as well.

Sharing my testimony at the direction of God during the timing of God was an answer to many people's prayers. I am using my experience to touch the lives of people on various continents throughout the world. Had I not obeyed God, I don't know how many lives would be untouched.

I believe everything has a season. In this season, my assignment is to continue traveling to share the word of my testimony about the healing grace and power of God while living a faith life before people.

My testimony taught me how to embrace my scars, my crooked smile, and my removable teeth I must keep clean every day. I would not have it any other way. I am a CANCER SURVIVOR THROUGH FAITH!

Photos of current life:

ABOUT THE AUTHOR

Sarah Elisabeth Anderson, the youngest of three children, was born in Indianola Mississippi to Leroy and Carol Washington Anderson. Sarah, whose name means "Princess Consecrated to God", was brought up in the church and was taught to always trust God in everything. In 2000, Sarah and her mother relocated to Chicago. Since coming to Chicago, Sarah has stolen the hearts of most of her teachers, principals, and even her Pastor, Superintendent Michael Eaddy. Her genuine spirit and love for God often draws others to her without a sweat.

Chosen, by Reverend Jesse L. Jackson and Rainbow PUSH, Sarah traveled to Ghana, West Africa in 2008, an experience that would change her life forever. It was there where the Lord began to deal with her about her own life in the United States and how He wanted to use her. Although she did not understand exactly how the Lord would use her, she accepted the challenge.

In 2009, a graduating senior and 4 months pregnant, Sarah began to experience pain in her body. Her mother took her to the doctor time after time after time. In June 2009, the pain was so excruciating, Sarah convinced her mother to change doctors. It was in December 2009, Sarah would receive a diagnosis that rocked her entire world – STAGE 4 head and neck cancer. In October 2010, after going through extensive treatment and reconstruction, Sarah would receive a prognosis of CANCER FREE.

Although the odds were seemingly stacked against her, Thornton Township High School administration, counseling team, and teachers ensured Sarah would be able to receive her high school diploma despite not being able to complete her senior year. She was unable to fully walk or be subjected to the heat of the sun. However, in May 2010, Thornton Township came to pick her up, drove her across the football stadium so she could receive her high school diploma. Today, Sarah is a junior majoring in secondary math education at Grand Canyon University online. She is working on completing her book entitled Cancer Survivor Through Faith. In this writing, she will detail all of the miraculous aspects of her battle with cancer as a teenager and a young mother. She has been gifted to write songs that the Lord gives and will be soon completing her single entitled "I Made It Through". The message behind the music is simply awesome.

She has a passion to help as many people as she possibly can while upholding a standard of holiness and righteous living. Sarah is committed to share with the world how the Lord used this disease to change her life for the better. She is committed to ministering to those who need to hear a message of hope, healing, inspiration, and FAITH in GOD. Sarah realizes that her healing came only through her relationship to God and her willingness to KEEP THE FAITH.

Sarah is the mother of her miracle child, Navayah L'Faith Mayfield, without whom, the progression of the cancer may not have been realized as quickly... She credits her FAITH in GOD for her TOTAL HEALING...

Printed in the United States
By Bookmasters